Original title:
The Power of a Praying Wife

Copyright © 2024 Book Fairy Publishing
All rights reserved.

Editor: Theodor Taimla
Author: Samira Siil
ISBN HARDBACK: 978-9916-756-94-2
ISBN PAPERBACK: 978-9916-756-95-9

Radiance of Her Plea

In the quiet of the night,
Amidst the stars' gleaming sea,
Softly whispered, pure and bright,
Echoes the radiance of her plea.

Eyes that hold the morning dew,
Tears unshed yet filled with grace,
Begging love as skies turn blue,
Carving dreams in endless space.

With each word, a moonlit dance,
Promises like fireflies,
Glowing hints of sweet romance,
Beneath the vast celestial skies.

Beyond the reach of earthly binds,
Her voice crafts the starlit tale,
In her plea, the universe finds,
Wishes woven, hopes unveil.

So in the still, where shadows lie,
Trust in whispers, heart set free,
For in her call, love will comply,
Awakened by her radiant plea.

Faithful Whispering

In the hush of twilight's glow,
Softly whispers faith, so low;
Guiding hearts through darkened night,
Promising the morning light.

In the quiet of the dawn,
Faithful whisper carries on;
Leading souls through trials grave,
Showing paths to hearts so brave.

In the midst of life's great storm,
Faithful whispers keep us warm;
Holding hands through highs and lows,
Binding hearts where love still flows.

Silent Intercessions

In silence, prayer takes flight,
Through the shadows, into light;
Every word, though unspoken,
Heals the hearts that are broken.

Through the stillness, voices rise,
Silent pleas that touch the skies;
Whispered wishes, pure and bright,
Hope is kindled in the night.

Silent intercessions chime,
Beyond the grasp of space and time;
Linking souls in quiet grace,
In the sacred, timeless place.

Sacred Devotion

In the chapel's quiet peace,
There devotion finds release;
Hearts aligned with heavens' call,
Humbled souls begin to fall.

Candles flicker, shadows play,
Sacred words by night and day;
Every breath a prayer profound,
Sacred vows in silence bound.

True devotion, deep and pure,
Spirit's touch that's always sure;
In this space, the soul reveals,
Sacred love that never yields.

Heartfelt Petitions

Heartfelt prayers like rivers flow,
From the depths where sorrows grow;
Every sigh and whispered plea,
Carries love across the sea.

Petitions rise to skies so high,
Heartfelt whispers never die;
Seeking grace in moments bleak,
Healing strength when we are weak.

Heartfelt cries in faith, we send,
To the heavens, love extend;
In the silence, we confide,
Spirit walks here by our side.

Faithful Murmurs

In twilight's gentle, soft embrace,
The whispers of the night unfold,
A chorus sung in silent grace,
Of stories new and promises old.

Among the stars, a murmured psalm,
Faith's gentle breath upon the air,
A beacon bright, a soothing calm,
In shadows deep, it finds us there.

The moon's sweet glow, a tender guide,
Leads hearts towards the morning light,
In every tear, where sorrows bide,
Faith blooms anew, dispelling fright.

Heavenly Shield

Beneath the arc of endless skies,
A shield divine, unseen yet near,
With gentle hands it sanctifies,
And banishes our every fear.

Against the tempest, ever strong,
It holds us safe through darkest nights,
A sacred bond where we belong,
In tender care, it sets things right.

Through valleys deep and mountains tall,
This heavenly armor stands the test,
In every rise and every fall,
A guard that grants us peace and rest.

Whispers of Hope

In morning's kiss, a promise born,
The whisper of a brand-new day,
Where shadows flee and light adorn,
The path where weary hearts can stray.

In gentle breezes soft and kind,
The whispers lift, a hopeful song,
To fragile dreams once left behind,
They're carried forth, where they belong.

Through storm and rain, these murmurs rise,
To paint the sky with hues of gold,
A hopeful gleam in endless skies,
A vision bright, a truth retold.

Divine Assurance

Within the heart where doubts reside,
A voice of calm, so pure and clear,
It quiets storms that rage inside,
And turns despair to faith sincere.

With every step, divine pursuit,
A guiding hand, a steadfast friend,
It leads us to our strong repute,
And fortifies our wills to mend.

In trials faced and battles lost,
Its whisperings remain our guide,
No fear too great, no trial's cost,
For in this grace, we do abide.

Guardian's Prayer

Beneath the stars' eternal glow,
I whisper prayers, soft and low,
For strength to guard and light to show,
Within the night, through ebb and flow.

May shadows yield to morning bright,
And courage thrive through darkest night,
With every step, in wrong or right,
Guide me, Guardian, with your light.

In boundless skies where dreams take flight,
Watch over souls both near and tight,
Let love and peace their fears ignite,
And banish sorrow from their sight.

Heavenly Petition

In quiet hours of twilight's fold,
I raise a voice to heavens bold,
For mercy, grace, and peace untold,
As daylight fades and nights grow cold.

Let angels gather, wings unfurled,
To shield the fragile from this world,
In whispers soft, their wings are swirled,
In sacred dance, with love, impearled.

May faith unchain the weary heart,
And hope and healing a new start,
O heavenly host, play your part,
Answer this plea from lips apart.

Sacred Trust

In moments still, the vibe we trust,
In paths unseen, where hearts adjust,
Our spirits rise from earth's thin crust,
To love, to hope—a sacred trust.

With every breath the soul rekindles,
And doubts dissolve like morning spindles,
In bonds of faith, our hope enclasps,
Like sunlight through the dewy glass.

So hold this gift, this sacred thread,
By trust and love, let hearts be led,
For in each bond that we have sped,
Lies sacred truth, in whispers spread.

Bound by Faith

Amidst the storm, when tempests wail,
We anchor faith with steadfast sail,
No fear shall make our courage pale,
For love and trust, we shall prevail.

In every trial, a beacon's spark,
To guide us through the world so stark,
And in the night that feels so dark,
Our faith's bright glow shall leave its mark.

With hands entwined, hearts intertwined,
In faith, our souls are well aligned,
Bound by truth and love combined,
Eternal peace in us enshrined.

Divine Companionship

In gardens where the moonlight gleams,
Two souls entwined as one,
A dance of dreams beneath the beams,
Their journey just begun.

Whispered secrets in the night,
Stars bear silent witness,
Hearts aligned with pure delight,
In eternal bliss.

Hand in hand, they traverse time,
Bound by fate's sweet tether,
In love's pure and gentle rhyme,
They navigate together.

Guardian of Love

A heart so true, a love profound,
Protector of the flame,
Guiding light that knows no bound,
In passion with no name.

Shielding from the storm's embrace,
Defender of the heart,
In their arms, a sacred place,
Where true love's stories start.

Eyes that see the soul's intent,
With valor and with grace,
A guardian of love's ascent,
In life's eternal race.

Sacred Bonds

Entwined in fate, two spirits soar,
Beyond the realms of time,
Their hearts united evermore,
In love's transcendent climb.

Promises in whispered tones,
Secrets to none but night,
Their sacred bond, a union known,
A beacon pure and bright.

Through trials and through joys they stride,
In memories held dear,
Together they shall always bide,
With hearts sincere, they steer.

Hallowed Vows

Underneath a sky so vast,
With whispers of the breeze,
Vows of love forever cast,
Amidst the ancient trees.

Hands are clasped and hearts entwined,
In moments pure and true,
Promises that time defined,
In shades of every hue.

With every breath and solemn word,
In hallowed vows they stand,
Their love, a song that's always heard,
Across a timeless land.

Heaven's Outreach

Through clouds and stars, the light descends,
An embrace from realms unseen,
Whispers of hope the sky extends,
A bridge where souls convene.

In dreams, we touch the angel's hand,
Their presence warm and clear,
Guiding us through starlit land,
Banishing doubt and fear.

Mornings bloom with heaven's grace,
A symphony of gold,
Each day a chance, a newfound space,
For miracles to unfold.

Sacramental Unity

Candles flicker, rites commence,
In chambers old and grand,
Hearts in solemn reverence,
Behold the sacred band.

Chalice raised with sacred wine,
Consecrated bread,
In this moment, souls align,
By faith, forever fed.

Mysteries unfold anew,
In whispers and in psalms,
Through sacraments, our spirits grew,
In unity and calm.

Sacred Support

In every trial, a hidden guide,
A strength beyond the seen,
Through darkest valleys by our side,
A bond that's evergreen.

Encased in love's eternal clasp,
No storm can break the chain,
Through grace, we find a gentle grasp,
That washes away the pain.

In prayers spoken, silent cries,
Companions in the night,
Our faith uplifts and amplifies,
A beacon burning bright.

Eternal Blessings

In gardens where the flowers bloom,
A scent of heaven's kiss,
Soft whispers in the morning's loom,
Bring everlasting bliss.

Each moment rich with blessings fair,
A promise from above,
Eternity in every prayer,
A testament of love.

Life's tapestry of blessings sown,
With threads of grace and light,
In every heart, a seed is grown,
To guide us through the night.

Mystic Bond

In moonlit nights, where shadows play,
Our souls unite in dance and sway.
A silent pledge, a silent bond,
In whispered winds, in lakes beyond.

Through dreams that weave the starry sky,
A mystic thread that never dies.
Together still, though far apart,
This bond we share, heart to heart.

Prayerful Heart

In dawn's first light, a humble plea,
With whispered hopes upon the sea.
A heart that yearns, a soul that seeks,
In prayerful moments, solace speaks.

Through silent nights and stormy gales,
A prayerful heart forever prevails.
With quiet strength and endless faith,
In every prayer, God's love is graced.

Holy Intercession

In sacred spaces, candles gleam,
Where whispered prayers form a stream.
In these moments, pure and still,
Holy intercession meets our will.

Guardian spirits, voices strong,
Carry our pleadings, ever long.
In faith we trust, in hope we wait,
For holy intercession at heaven's gate.

Divine Petitions

Beneath the starlit skies, I kneel in prayer,
Whispering dreams into the midnight air,
With every plea, my heart's affections flow,
Seeking a light in darkness, to bestow.

From heavens high, a gentle breeze descends,
Carrying hopes, where mortal wishes blend,
In silent faith, I cast my fears away,
Trusting divine hands to mold the clay.

For every tear, a whisper soft and mild,
In cosmic arms, I'm cradled like a child,
Each longing breath, a hymn of sacred sound,
In these divine petitions, grace is found.

Serene Strength

In quiet valleys, where the lilies rest,
A strength serene blooms gently in my chest,
Through trials hard, and nights of endless gloom,
Resilience springs, an everlasting bloom.

Among the shadows, courage softly gleams,
In whispered winds, and in my quiet dreams,
An inner flame, unwavering and pure,
A steadfast heart, in hopefulness secure.

Within the storm, I find my anchored peace,
With every wave, my resolve finds release,
For in the depths, my strength is carved and formed,
A fortress bold, amidst life's raging storm.

Celestial Accord

In night's embrace, where stars align with grace,
A cosmic dance unfolds in endless space,
Each twinkling light, a note in heaven's score,
A symphony, that echoes evermore.

The moonlight weaves a tapestry so bright,
In silver threads, it binds the realms of night,
With every beat, a harmony is born,
A celestial accord, from dusk till morn.

Through endless skies, where galaxies unite,
A peaceful chord resounds, serene and bright,
In cosmic choir, we find our place and part,
In this grand song, we hear the universe's heart.

Spiritual Fortitude

In quiet solitude, firm faith arises,
A spiritual strength, that never disguises,
With every trial, my spirit finds its voice,
In paths of light, my heart will always rejoice.

Through endless battles, courage finds its ground,
In whispers soft, a mighty roar is found,
My soul, a fortress, standing tall and true,
With inner peace, in every storm I grew.

For every step, a beacon lights my way,
In darkened times, it turns the night to day,
With steadfast grace, my fortitude endures,
In soulful faith, my spirit's strength ensures.

Faithful Advocate

In shadows deep, your voice does rise,
A guiding hand 'neath starlit skies.
You whisper truths that soothe the soul,
A beacon bright when nights are cold.

Your presence near, a sturdy shield,
In every storm, you make me yield.
I trust your light to lead the way,
Through darkened paths to break of day.

A steadfast friend in life's grand show,
Through valleys low, to heights we go.
With every prayer and quiet plea,
Your strength and grace encompass me.

Angelic Echoes

Soft whispers float on evening breeze,
Like gentle songs from ancient seas.
In dreams they come, those angel's calls,
A timeless dance as starlight falls.

In moments still, when silence reigns,
Their echoes chase away the pains.
Each note a balm, each word a cheer,
These heavenly hymns draw us near.

Through endless night and dawning day,
In every step, they're here to stay.
Angelic echoes fill the heart,
A sacred gift, we're never apart.

Heavenly Watch

Above the clouds, a watchful eye,
Through day and night, it sweeps the sky.
With tender care, it guards the realm,
A captain at the twilight's helm.

In every hour, through joy and woe,
Its vigil keeps, through sun and snow.
Guiding souls with gentle might,
It finds each heart in darkest night.

Unceasing gaze, so pure and clear,
It hears each hope, it knows each tear.
O steadfast watch, in heavens true,
We rest secure, held safe by you.

Devout Heart

In quiet pews where shadows rest,
A fervent prayer, a soul confessed.
With humble heart and hands entwined,
Faith and hope in spirits bind.

Through trials deep and joys so grand,
A devout heart does firmly stand.
In every beat, a love that's true,
A guiding flame for me and you.

O'er every hill, through every vale,
A devout heart shall never fail.
With steadfast step and gaze so clear,
It walks with faith, unbowed by fear.

Heavenward Hopes

In twilight's glow, we gaze afar,
With dreams alight, like a guiding star,
Through whispered winds, our spirits soar,
To realms where time can touch no more.

Amidst the clouds, where angels sing,
We cast our hopes on feathered wing,
To seek the place where hearts unite,
Beyond the veil of endless night.

With every step on earthly ground,
In echoes faint, heaven's call is found,
A beacon shining, pure and true,
Guiding souls to skies anew.

In silent prayers and heartfelt pleas,
Our hopes ascend on tender breeze,
To where the heavens gently part,
And light illuminates each heart.

Through trials faced and shadows past,
We hold our faith, our hopes steadfast,
For in the heavens, love's embrace,
Awaits us in that sacred place.

Eternal Vigil

Beneath the moon's soft, silvery light,
The guardians keep their watch by night,
With eyes that gleam like stars above,
They guard the ones they dearly love.

Their presence felt in whispers low,
In shadows cast by candle's glow,
Through endless time, they stand so near,
Dispelling darkness, calming fear.

With silent steps and unseen grace,
They wander through each secret place,
And in the hearts they cherish most,
Their gentle touch is ever close.

Through storm and still, they do not tire,
Their vigil fueled by love's own fire,
Protecting dreams and soothing pain,
Till dawn returns to wakeful plane.

In moments stretched through timeless span,
The vigilant form a steadfast clan,
In bonds unbroken, pure and fine,
A love eternal, hands entwine.

Spiritual Embrace

In tender whispers, spirits blend,
Where earthly prayers to heavens send,
A touch beyond the veil of night,
In love's embrace, pure, infinite.

Through life's complexities and woes,
A gentle presence softly flows,
To cradle hearts with boundless care,
And lift the burdens they must bear.

In quiet moments, peace descends,
And anguish finds its rightful end,
For in the arms of spirit's grace,
We find the strength to face each place.

With every breath, a sacred bond,
Between the here and the beyond,
Is woven tight, a golden thread,
Connecting souls, though paths have spread.

As day to night, and night to day,
In love's embrace, we find our way,
For spirits, bound by faith, will rise,
Together, ever, to the skies.

Celestial Conversations

Beneath the stars, in twilight's gleam,
We share our thoughts, our hopes, our dreams,
And voices blend in cosmic choir,
Igniting hearts with heaven's fire.

In whispers soft, and laughter sweet,
Celestial voices gently greet,
The night, a canvas, vast and wide,
Where dreams and wonders dare to glide.

Through constellations' ancient lore,
We seek the truths forevermore,
In dialogues that time transcends,
We find where soul and cosmos blend.

Each word a light, each thought a star,
Guiding us from near to far,
A conversation through the night,
With cosmos in harmonious flight.

As dawn approaches, night's retreat,
Our hearts with celestial love replete,
For in each word, each silent sigh,
We touch the heavens, sky to sky.

Whispers in the Meadow

Amidst the blooms and emerald green,
A whispered breeze, a sight unseen,
Soft voices rise and gently fold,
A meadow's secrets, manifold.

Sunlight dances, shadows play,
In twilight's soft and fleeting sway,
A symphony of life unfolds,
Stories that the meadow holds.

Flower petals kiss the air,
Nature's whispers, sweetly fair,
Crickets sing and owls entrain,
Echoes in the growing grain.

Streams of silver, trickling light,
Weaving tales in lunar night,
Mysteries in whispers saved,
In meadow's heart, so deeply engraved.

Footsteps tender, lovers' dreams,
In this meadow, 'neath sunbeams,
Hearts align and spirits glean,
In whispers soft, unseen, serene.

Soul's Gentle Petition

In silent murmurs, hearts profess,
A soul's petition, soft caress,
Glimmers in the quiet night,
Seeking solace, pure delight.

Beneath the arch of twilight's hue,
The soul's desires come into view,
A plea for peace where shadows roam,
In hearts, the call for love, a home.

Gentle whispers, carried far,
By moon's embrace and distant star,
Unveiling dreams, a truth confessed,
In silent night, a soul addressed.

Voices merge in whispered prayer,
A symphony beyond compare,
Each gentle note, a soul's pure plea,
In unity, they seek to be.

Beneath the calm of evening's spell,
The heart's soft whispers rise and swell,
In gentle petition, souls align,
In echoes of the heart, divine.

A Wife's Sacred Plea

In quiet nights, the heart does yearn,
With every star, for love's return,
A plea so sacred, whispered low,
In tender words that gently flow.

She stands by windows wrapped in dreams,
Where moonlight casts its silver beams,
A wife, in love's eternal plea,
For hands to hold, for hearts set free.

Her voice, a tender, soft refrain,
Calls out across the midnight plain,
Hopes and fears in whispers blend,
A sacred prayer for love to mend.

Bound by vows they once did take,
She pleads with stars for heart's sake,
In every breath, a sacred plea,
To bind their souls eternally.

In shadows deep and silence wrought,
Her plea for love, with hopes fraught,
Echoes through the night's embrace,
A wife's devotion, full of grace.

Evening Benedictions

As dusk descends, a hush so deep,
The world prepares for night's sweet sleep,
Evening's grace, in gentle light,
Bestows its calm, serene delight.

Stars awaken, softly gleam,
Beneath the heavens' tranquil seam,
Whispers of the day now passed,
In evening's quiet, shadows cast.

Moonlight's blessing, pure and kind,
Soothes the restless, peace to find,
In benedictions softly said,
Laying worries, tired heads.

Cool breezes sing with tender care,
A lullaby in twilight's air,
Blessings on the world bestowed,
In evening's gentle, calming code.

Night's embrace, so soft and wise,
Cradles earth 'neath starry skies,
In evening benedictions dear,
Whispers of peace for hearts to hear.

Sanctuary of Whispers

In the hush of ancient groves,
Where secrets softly lie,
The wind through leaves it roves,
    A graceful lullaby.

Among the mossy stones,
Whispers weave and wind,
Stories etched in bone,
Of ages left behind.

Beneath the silvered moon,
Shadows gently dance,
A sanctuary soon,
Lost in twilight trance.

Where dreams and echoes meet,
And silence sings a tune,
In this hidden retreat,
We find our reverie soon.

With each breath we take,
In this hallowed, quiet air,
New life from whispers wake,
A place beyond compare.

Ribboned in Blessings

Threads of dawn unwound,
In soft and golden hue,
Blessings all around,
In morning's gentle view.

Each day a gift anew,
Wrapped in silken light,
With every color true,
Ascending into night.

Tapestries of hope,
We weave with every breath,
In dreams we learn to cope,
With life, with love, with death.

Hearts tied in love's embrace,
Ribboned in blessings bright,
We move with tender grace,
Through darkness into light.

In fields where joy is sown,
And laughter freely flows,
We see how love has grown,
In life's eternal rows.

Her Heavenly Armor

She dons the morning light,
As armor pure and bright,
With grace in every stride,
She conquers with her might.

Her gaze, a beacon strong,
In the darkest night's refrain,
Through trials all day long,
Her courage will sustain.

Her heart, a fortress grand,
Built with love and care,
No storm can seize the land,
Of strength that she lays bare.

Each step, a warrior's call,
In battles she must fight,
No foe can make her fall,
She stands, a boundless light.

With heaven by her side,
And armor shining gold,
In her, the stars confide,
A story yet untold.

Vows Beyond the Veil

In twilight's tender glow,
Where shadows softly sway,
Two hearts together grow,
In love that finds its way.

Beyond the world's embrace,
Beneath a sky so pale,
They meet in sacred grace,
And whisper vows beyond the veil.

Through ages and through tears,
Their spirits intertwine,
In moments lost to years,
Their love remains divine.

Oaths whispered in the night,
With stars to bear their plight,
They journey into light,
As one through endless flight.

In silence and in song,
Their bond will never fail,
For love, so pure and strong,
Lives on beyond the veil.

Believe and Trust

In the quiet hum of dawn,
When night surrenders to day,
A whisper of hope is drawn,
Guiding hearts on their way.

Through shadows dense and long,
With courage they entwine,
Belief and trust grow strong,
In harmony divine.

Mountains tall they climb,
Rivers wild they cross,
With faith, they transcend time,
No journey is a loss.

In moments fleeting, tender,
Where dreams like stars ignite,
Souls to love surrender,
In trust, they find their light.

So hold close, dear beliefs,
Let trust be your guide,
In life's profound reliefs,
They walk side by side.

Faith's Armor

Against the winds of doubt,
A shield so pure and bright,
Faith's armor wraps about,
Turning gloom into light.

In battles tough and long,
Where shadows often play,
A heart with faith beats strong,
And night turned into day.

Each scar tells a story,
Of courage, fierce and bold,
Faith in its silent glory,
Is worth its weight in gold.

Through storms that howl and rage,
Through trials that test our soul,
Faith turns every page,
Making broken pieces whole.

Stand tall in faith's true might,
Let courage be your song,
For in its radiant light,
We find where we belong.

Vows to Heaven

Under star-kissed skies,
With vows as pure as snow,
Promises rise and tie,
In love's eternal glow.

Hearts entwined in grace,
By destiny aligned,
Each vow in Heaven's space,
Is endlessly enshrined.

In whispers soft and kind,
In hands forever clasped,
Faith and love combined,
With bonds that hold so fast.

Through every storm we'll sail,
On love's celestial sea,
Our vows they shall prevail,
In sacred unity.

To heavens we declare,
Our love, our solemn trust,
In vows beyond compare,
Forever more, we must.

Graceful Guardianship

In the tender moonlit night,
Where angels spread their wings,
Guardians shine so bright,
With grace that softly sings.

Each step they gently guide,
Through shadows of the wild,
With them by our side,
Our hearts are reconciled.

Whispers in the rain,
Their love a sacred shield,
Through joy and through pain,
Their wisdom is revealed.

With hands that lift us high,
Above the trials we face,
They carry us to the sky,
In warm, embracing grace.

So honor them with love,
These spirits pure and true,
Like stars in skies above,
They always see us through.

Celestial Bond

In twilight's gentle embrace, stars confide,
Eternal stories in the heavens wide.
Cosmic whispers of an ageless tale,
Beyond the night's ethereal veil.

A bond unspoken, yet deeply felt,
Through cosmic strings, our souls have knelt.
Celestial rhythms, heartbeats align,
In the vast expanse, our spirits shine.

Galaxies dance in a silent trance,
Timeless steps in an eternal romance.
Their luminescence guides us all,
In every rise, in every fall.

Infinite space, yet we belong,
In the universe's ancient song.
Boundless love in starlit skies,
A bond that never fades nor dies.

Eternal stars, keep your watch,
Over our hearts, a sacred notch.
For in the night, when we glance above,
We find solace in celestial love.

Beacon of Faith

Through the tempest, through the storm,
A beacon of faith keeps us warm.
Guiding light in darkest night,
A promise in the faintest light.

In trials deep, in shadows long,
Faith remains steadfast and strong.
Beyond the doubt, beyond the fear,
A whisper that we're always near.

When paths diverge, uncertain, vast,
Faithful hearts will hold them fast.
Every step, in trust we take,
A stronger bond, in faith, we make.

Hope endures through endless days,
In faith's unyielding, brilliant rays.
Guard against the darkest plight,
A beacon shining ever bright.

In each soul, this light does dwell,
An inner strength, a silent swell.
Through life's journey, faith will lead,
A guiding star in every need.

Whispered Prayers for You

In the hush of dawn's first light,
Whispered prayers take their flight.
Gentle words in morning dew,
Quietly, they're sent for you.

Through the day, when shadows grow,
Unseen blessings start to flow.
Carried on the wings of hope,
With each whisper, strength to cope.

Evening falls, stars softly shine,
Prayers remain a sacred line.
In the silence, heartbeats say,
Words of love to guide your way.

Night enfolds, dreams take flight,
Whispered prayers in moon's soft light.
Guardians in the silent night,
Holding you, till morning bright.

Ever present, unseen care,
In whispered prayers, always there.
For you, my heart does ever plead,
May you find all that you need.

In Faithful Silence

In the quiet, a promise stands,
Silent whispers clasped in hands.
Faith resides in hush profound,
Silent moments, without sound.

Vows unspoken, trust conveyed,
In this silence, hearts displayed.
Beyond the noise, in stillness deep,
Faithful secrets, silent keep.

Through life's tumult, voices loud,
Faithful silence stands unbowed.
In the calm, a bond does form,
In quiet strength, hearts stay warm.

Words unneeded, presence speaks,
Silent gestures, moments seek.
In the stillness, love extends,
Faithful silence never bends.

Here we stand, no words to share,
In faith's silence, we're laid bare.
Holding close this silent trust,
Faithful silence, hearts adjust.

Holy Devotion

In dawn's first light, a whisper calls,
A prayerful breeze through hallowed halls,
Hearts uplift, in faith unshaken,
Spirits soar, in grace awakened.

Eyes cast skyward, souls entwined,
In sacred bond, our hearts aligned,
Steps of purpose, path of light,
In holy devotion, day and night.

Chorus of angels, hymns resound,
In worship's realm, we stay unbound,
Hands together, hope embraced,
In divine love, forever graced.

Candles flicker, shadows fade,
In reverence, our fears allayed,
Whispered vows, in solemn tone,
In holy devotion, we're never alone.

Beneath the stars, in twilight's hush,
A silent prayer, a blissful blush,
Eternal light, our guide and friend,
In holy devotion, till the end.

Heavenly Vigil

Under moonlit skies, we stand,
With hearts aglow, and lanterns planned,
A sacred watch, beneath the stars,
In silent prayer, no worldly bars.

Glistening eyes, in night's embrace,
A heavenly vigil, our faith's trace,
Whispers soar, on winds so tall,
In divine presence, we hear the call.

Shadows dance, as spirits meld,
In quiet union, our fears dispelled,
Eternal promise, keeps us near,
In heavenly vigil, love sincere.

Celestial gaze, we never part,
With every breath, a hopeful heart,
In this vigil, our souls unite,
Guided by the holy light.

With dawn's first break, our spirits rise,
A new day born, in celestial eyes,
In bonds unbroken, faith renews,
In heavenly vigil, grace ensues.

Blessed Unity

Together in the warmth of love,
With blessings showered from above,
Hand in hand, our hearts declared,
In blessed unity, we're paired.

Echoes of laughter, joys untold,
In sacred bond, our souls unfold,
With shared dreams, and whispered prayers,
In blessed unity, no despairs.

Eyes reflect a future bright,
In the glow of trust and light,
With every step, our spirits blend,
In blessed unity, till the end.

Gentle touches, passions soar,
In unity, we stand secure,
Bound by faith, with skies so blue,
In blessed unity, pure and true.

Through trials faced and victories won,
Our journey shines, like morning sun,
In every moment, near and far,
In blessed unity, just as we are.

Gentle Conversations

In the quiet of a peaceful night,
Whispers soft, as stars ignite,
Gentle words, like falling rain,
In conversations, hearts refrain.

Eyes meet eyes, in silent song,
Exchanging thoughts where souls belong,
With every breath, a world unveiled,
In gentle conversations, love prevailed.

Hearts aligned in sacred space,
In whispered dreams, we find our place,
Unseen rivers, flowing free,
In gentle conversations, you and me.

Hands entwined, we journey far,
In spoken word, no need for par,
A dance of minds, a shared refrain,
In gentle conversations, joy and pain.

Under moon and sky so vast,
We share our truths, in shadows cast,
With each exchange, connection deep,
In gentle conversations, peace we keep.

Sacred Watch

Beneath the silent evening sky,
The stars commence their radiant show,
Through timeless sentinels on high,
A sacred watch, as ages flow.

Whispered winds in midnight's veil,
Carry secrets of the night,
In shadows where the spirits sail,
Mystic dance in silver light.

Guided by the lunar beam,
Wanderers in dreams unite,
Starlight threads the silent seam,
Crafting tales of pure delight.

Each heartbeat in the cosmos loud,
Echoes through the velvet sphere,
Woven in the astral shroud,
Souls encircle, drawing near.

Eternal in its ancient cast,
The heavens keep their watch on high,
In every moment, future past,
The sacred watch, a lasting tie.

Gentle Supplications

In quiet moments of the dawn,
When night gives way to tender light,
Through whispers of a waking yawn,
We find our strength in morning's sight.

With hands that fold in earnest plea,
And hearts that seek the purest grace,
We offer gentle supplications free,
In silent prayer, a sacred space.

Let hope be stirred in every breath,
And kindness flow from heart to hand,
In facing life, defying death,
With love as guide, let peace expand.

Through trials that darken weary mind,
And burdens that our souls confound,
Within these hymns, our paths aligned,
To solace in each word profound.

Unseen, the powers gently heed,
Our whispers, lifted to the skies,
In faith, we plant the smallest seed,
And trust it grows, our hearts' replies.

Binding Faith

In darkest times, through storm and strife,
A light persists, a beacon bright,
It guides us through the perils rife,
With binding faith, in darkest night.

When doubts assail our weary mind,
And fears arise, obscure our view,
A steadfast trust is there to find,
Binding faith, our strength renew.

Through valleys deep and mountains tall,
In shadows cast by looming fates,
We stand as one, unbowed by all,
Binding faith our bond creates.

Within each heart a flame is kept,
A fire that no storm can quell,
In unity, our fears we've swept,
Binding faith in us does dwell.

Together as the days unfold,
In trust, we face the unknown quest,
With binding faith, our stories told,
In unity, we've been blessed.

Heartfelt Meditations

In silent folds of morning's light,
We find a space for calm to bloom,
Through heartfelt meditations bright,
Our spirits cleanse, dispelling gloom.

Each breath becomes a gentle prayer,
A touch of peace on troubled soul,
In moments free of worldly care,
We seek and find ourselves whole.

In stillness deep, where thoughts repose,
Unravelled from the day's demands,
We drift where quiet waters flow,
Held gently in serenity's hands.

With open heart and mind attuned,
We listen to the whispering air,
In quietude, we are cocooned,
And burdens lifted, light as prayer.

As dawn unfurls its golden stream,
We rise renewed, with visions clear,
Through heartfelt meditations' dream,
We walk in peace, dispelling fear.

Unseen Strength

Beneath the surface, dormant lies,
A power hidden from the eyes,
In quiet shadows, whispers trace,
The unseen strength of boundless grace.

Through darkest trials, hearts endure,
With steadfast courage, pure and sure,
Resilience blooms in silent tides,
Unseen strength from deep inside.

In whispered winds, resolve stands tall,
A silent guardian through it all,
Though unseen, it holds the sky,
With roots deep set, it can't deny.

In gentle hearts, it weaves its thread,
A force that guides where fears are fed,
Unseen strength, forever near,
A silent grace that conquers fear.

Each step, unknown, yet still you find,
The hidden power intertwined,
Unseen strength, a quiet roar,
A guiding light forevermore.

Heavenly Comfort

In twilight's hush, a solace found,
Where heavens whisper soft around,
A tender glow, a starry weave,
Heavenly comfort, hearts believe.

On moonlit paths, where shadows cease,
A gentle touch, a quiet peace,
Celestial hands that cradle night,
Heavenly comfort's guiding light.

Amid the dreams of silent skies,
A lullaby from angel's sighs,
Embrace of stars, a loving thread,
Heavenly comfort for the dread.

When tear-filled eyes seek solace warm,
In softest folds of love's own form,
A tender kiss, from realms above,
Heavenly comfort, purest love.

In stillness, hearts are gently swayed,
By whispers of the night's cascade,
Heavenly comfort softly sings,
A peace that only heaven brings.

Devout Promises

In sacred vows, our hearts align,
With words that stretch, beyond all time,
A promise made, a solemn bond,
Devout through life, and far beyond.

Each dawn renews the pledge we swear,
In whispered prayers, in tender care,
Through trials faced, and joys we find,
Our devout promises entwined.

In faith, we build, a future bright,
With love as guide, and truth as light,
Through shadows cast by doubt and fear,
Devout promises draw us near.

With every breath, commitment grows,
A trust that only true love knows,
In deepest hearts, the vows remain,
Devout promises, free of stain.

As time unfolds, the journey's grace,
In every step, our vows embrace,
Devout promises, ever strong,
A sacred bond, where we belong.

Hallowed Covering

Beneath the stars, a veil of night,
A hallowed covering, pure delight,
In whispers soft, and shadows deep,
A sacred silence, angels keep.

The world below in silent breath,
Enfolded in a holy depth,
A shroud of calm, a peace profound,
In hallowed covering, grace is found.

In twilight's realm, where spirits drift,
A gentle touch, a sacred gift,
Each heart beneath, in solace held,
By hallowed covering, all fears dispelled.

Through storms that rage and trials fierce,
A shield of light that none can pierce,
In quietude, we find our stay,
Hallowed covering, night and day.

In every soul, this truth abides,
A shelter where the spirit hides,
With hallowed covering, we're blessed,
In sacred peace, our hearts find rest.

Echoes of Faith

In quiet woods, where shadows play,
Whispers of grace, both night and day.
Among the trees, prayers softly rise,
Towards a sky with endless skies.

Candles flicker, in sacred night,
Guiding hearts towards the light.
In each breath, an echoed plea,
Faith's gentle tune, eternally.

Rivers flow with humble song,
In their currents, faith belongs.
Mountains stand with reverent grace,
Nature's hymn, in this holy space.

Echoes of faith, in every leaf,
Bringing solace, easing grief.
Birds sing hymns, in twilight's fade,
Praising life in a blessed cascade.

In each moment, faith resounds,
In silent prayers, in joyful sounds.
Echoes linger, hearts embrace,
In sacred harmony, in divine grace.

Heaven's Grace

Across the sky, a golden hue,
Blessings from above, ever true.
In the dawn, light softly breaks,
Heaven's grace in morning's wakes.

Angels whisper, winds reply,
Songs of hope that never die.
In each star, a twinkling guide,
Heaven's grace, ever beside.

Softly spoken, in twilight's glow,
Divine mercy, hearts will know.
In each breath, a peaceful trace,
Of heaven's ever-present grace.

Rain that falls in gentle streams,
Carries with it, sacred dreams.
In each droplet, love's embrace,
Heaven's grace, in every place.

From dawn to dusk, within our view,
A tapestry of love so true.
Heaven's grace, in time and space,
Eternal, boundless, full of grace.

Faithful Guardians

By our side, in shadows deep,
Faithful guardians, their vigil keep.
Guiding steps, through night and day,
Helping light the righteous way.

Whispers in the silent night,
Steady hearts in battles' plight.
Shielding softly, unseen hands,
Faithful guardians, through life's demands.

Wings enfold with gentle care,
In their presence, we're aware.
Of love that spans both near and far,
Faithful guardians, just where we are.

In each trial, in each test,
They provide their quietest best.
Strength to carry, hope to lend,
Faithful guardians 'til the end.

Comfort found in their embrace,
In every moment, every place.
Faithful guardians, ever true,
Watching over in all we do.

Sacred Reflections

In still waters, mirrored skies,
Sacred reflections, where truth lies.
Gaze within, the soul's deep well,
In these quiet depths, divinity dwells.

Leaves that fall in gentle breeze,
Whispers carried from ancient trees.
Each one holds a timeless tale,
Sacred reflections, in nature's vale.

Sunset's glow on placid lake,
Dreams arise as daylight breaks.
In these moments, hearts unveil,
Secrets kept in sacred trail.

Reflections hold what words conceal,
Echoes of a world that's real.
In the quiet, in the pause,
Sacred reflections without flaws.

In every glance, in every sigh,
A hint of beauty passing by.
In reflections, truths we find,
Sacred insights to remind.

Dawn's Seraphic Whisper

The morning sun unfurls its ray,
Bright tendrils stretch, heralding day.
In whispered tones, the angels sing,
With hope and light, anew they bring.

Feathers dust the sky so blue,
Wings ascend where spirits flew.
Shrouded mist and dreams elope,
In dawn's embrace, we find our hope.

Golden threads weave through the air,
Glistening paths, a sacred prayer.
Silent voices, pure and sweet,
In dawn's seraphic, hearts then meet.

Softly gleams the world anew,
Morning dew on petals' hue.
In tranquil moments, gently kissed,
Seraphic whispers, none resist.

Each heartbeat syncs with daybreak's call,
Life awakens, standing tall.
In sacred light, we feel the shift,
A dawn's whisper, heaven's gift.

Mystic Faith's Bond

In twilight's gleam, a canvas pure,
Faith's mystic bond does endure.
An unseen tether, spirit ties,
Woven threads, within the skies.

Distant realms where heartbeats cling,
Muted hymns we softly sing.
Trust entwined in silent grace,
Mystic faith does time embrace.

Symbols etched in cosmic lore,
Wisdom ancient, to explore.
Through the veils, the seekers find,
In faith's grasp, the heart aligned.

Ethereal light where shadows cease,
Moments steeped in tranquil peace.
Mystic bond, forever fused,
In faith's essence, love suffused.

Whispers of the old and wise,
Guiding ship through tempest cries.
Bound by dreams and starry sea,
In faith's mystic, souls are free.

Anchor of Benediction

In tempest's heart, where wild winds howl,
Stands an anchor, firm and foul.
A prayerful hold, through storm and night,
Benediction's guiding light.

Mighty chains of hope's embrace,
Binding hearts in blessed grace.
Through the chaos and the cry,
An anchor holds beneath the sky.

Peace descends where turmoil roars,
Sanctity on distant shores.
Blessings flow in whispered psalm,
Anchor's strength, a soothing balm.

Souls adrift in churning sea,
Find their course through divinity.
Each wave a testament to core,
Anchored deep in sacred lore.

Eternal blessings, steadfast ground,
In benediction, hope is found.
Through life's trials and endless tides,
Anchor holds where faith abides.

Harmony in Hallowed Words

In sacred halls, where echoes dance,
Words like stars, in heaven's trance.
Harmony in hallowed speech,
In whispered tone, redemption's reach.

Verses cloaked in mystic lore,
Chorals swell and spirits soar.
Every phrase, a soul's delight,
In hallowed words, we find the light.

Melodies in sermons sung,
Every heart, with reverence, rung.
Sigils float on air so thin,
In sacred text, our truths begin.

Eons speak through ancient verse,
Time does bless and none reverse.
Harmony in righteous song,
With hallowed words, where we belong.

In the stillness of the mind,
Solace in each line we find.
Guided by the sacred script,
In hallowed words, our hearts equipped.

Soul's Whisper

In quiet nights, the soul speaks true,
Through dreams it weaves, the light breaks through.
A gentle call, from depths unknown,
In whispers, secrets softly shown.

Stars conspire, to guide our way,
In cosmic dance, the shadows sway.
Hearts align, in subtle grace,
A soulful whisper, time and space.

Silent echoes, through the heart,
A symphony, where feelings start.
Beyond the veil, where spirits tread,
In whispers, love is softly spread.

Through the winds, a timeless sound,
It lifts the soul, from earthly bound.
A whisper dear, a gentle flight,
With every breath, the soul ignites.

Mystic realms, where whispers lead,
The soul can trust, the heart will heed.
In hallowed halls, where whispers dwell,
The soul's own truth, its tale will tell.

Eternal Devotion

In the silence of the morn,
A love eternal, gently born.
Through fleeting days, and nights so cold,
A bond unbreakable, pure and bold.

With every breath, a promise made,
In shadows deep, where fears may fade.
An endless dance, in love's embrace,
Through trials faced, with strength and grace.

A heartbeat's vow, forever sworn,
In tempest nights, and weathers worn.
The timeless touch, of hand in hand,
In truth and trust, they firmly stand.

Beneath the vast and starlit skies,
Their love endures, it never dies.
A sacred flame, that brightly burns,
With every turn, to love returns.

In lifetime's span, through joy and strife,
Their love remains, the soul's own life.
Eternal devotion, pure and true,
A love that time can't bid adieu.

Loving Sentinel

Through darkest nights, and sunlit days,
A sentinel, in many ways.
With watchful eyes, and tender care,
A guardian, always there.

In every storm, and gentle breeze,
Their presence calms, the heart's unease.
A beacon bright, in love's own light,
A steadfast soul, through every fight.

With open arms, they stand awake,
Through trials faced, for love's own sake.
In every tear, and joyous cheer,
A sentinel to hold us near.

In endless love, their spirit binds,
The threads of life, in gentle kinds.
Through every path, they guide the way,
In silent strength, come night or day.

A loving heart, a watchful gaze,
Through all of time, and every phase.
In bonds so pure, they softly dwell,
A loving, faithful sentinel.

Heaven's Harmony

In angel's song, where dreams align,
A touch of grace, a note divine.
Through veils of light, and cosmic sea,
A harmony, in melody.

The heavens sing, a tranquil tune,
Beneath the sun, the stars, the moon.
With every chord, the heart expands,
In harmony, we join our hands.

A symphony, from skies above,
In every note, a breath of love.
The music swells, in tender waves,
A harmony, through lives it saves.

With gentle strings, and voices pure,
A timeless call, in love's allure.
The heavenly sound, it guides us near,
In harmony, we find no fear.

Through life's great song, in love's sweet chord,
In every sound, the soul restored.
A harmony, with heavens twine,
In music pure, our hearts align.

Angelic Pleas

In twilight's glow, I hear them seek,
Angelic pleas from heavens speak,
Graceful whispers in gentle breeze,
Hearts entwined with souls at ease.

Beneath the stars, their voices rise,
A chorus sweet fills up the skies,
Hope and love in purest form,
Guiding lost hearts through the storm.

Celestial lights our path define,
Through darkest nights, they intertwine,
Guardian wings of pure white light,
Comfort souls in silent night.

In dreams they come, in shadows fade,
Expectant dawn, their touch displayed,
Angelic pleas, a tender call,
Eternal love that binds us all.

Our hearts respond, in silence cry,
For angelic pleas transcend the sky,
A sacred bond we dare not sever,
A testament to love forever.

Soul's Cry

In depths of night, a soul's cry found,
Echoes through the hollow ground,
Yearning hearts, a mournful tone,
Seeking solace, never alone.

Beneath the moon's pale silver light,
Whispers blend with shadowed night,
A haunting plea, soft as a sigh,
From troubled souls, their voices fly.

Each tear a tale of sorrow's touch,
Of dreams once bright, now grieved so much,
In silence weep, in darkness find,
A soul's cry seeks a heart that's kind.

Beyond the stars, through veils unseen,
Hope and longing gently lean,
To grasp the dawn where hearts will mend,
A soul's cry waits for light to send.

When morning comes with warm embrace,
Dispelling night, leaving no trace,
A whispered prayer, a gentle breeze,
The soul's cry eased, now rests in peace.

Whispered Prayers

In quiet hours, when night is still,
Whispered prayers our hearts fulfill,
Softly spoken, carried high,
To unseen realms beyond the sky.

Through fragile hopes and tender fear,
These whispered prayers we hold so dear,
For healing light, for peace to come,
To mend the wounds that left us numb.

The stars bear witness to our plea,
In silent awe, they hear and see,
A universe that bends to hear,
The whispered prayers that draw us near.

In moments lost, in time's embrace,
We find within a sacred place,
Where whispered prayers meet heavens' ear,
And grace descends to dry the tear.

With every breath, a wish conveyed,
In whispered prayers, our hearts displayed,
A bond unbroken, softly traced,
In whispered prayers, we're gently graced.

Merciful Embrace

In times of woe, when hearts grow cold,
A merciful embrace unfolds,
Tender arms that hold us tight,
Through darkest hours, into light.

A comfort found in gentle sway,
To chase the shadows far away,
With every touch, a promise kept,
In merciful embrace, we've wept.

Beneath the weight of sorrow's crown,
This merciful embrace will drown,
All fears and doubts in warm cocoon,
To break the chains and heal the wound.

In silent halls where echoes play,
Their merciful embrace will stay,
A refuge from the storm's fierce cry,
To cradle hearts and lift us high.

With each new dawn, a fresh caress,
In merciful embrace, we bless,
Our lives renewed, our spirits freed,
By love's embrace, fulfilled in need.

Petitions in Bloom

In gardens of hope, where wishes take flight,
Whispers of dreams, both day and night.
Petals unfurl with desires so grand,
In the heart's gentle hush, close at hand.

With each budding blossom, a prayer is told,
Stories of love and of hearts ever bold.
Nature's own hymn in sunlight and rain,
Manifesting dreams, easing all pain.

Through meadows of faith, each bud gives way,
To colors of passion, a new hope today.
Where shadows of doubt fade into light,
Petitions in bloom, embracing the night.

Faith plants the seed in soft, tender ground,
In aspirations pure, true hopes are found.
Under celestial skies, bright stars align,
Petitions in bloom, dreams intertwine.

As springtime whispers secrets anew,
In fragrant testimony, wishes accrue.
Life's gentle flow in a vibrant tune,
Petitions in bloom, under the moon.

Steadfast Silent-Yearning

In the stillness of night, dreams softly stir,
Whispers of longing, in silence defer.
Hearts intertwined in the quiet refrain,
Bound by yearning, through joy and through pain.

Under twilight skies, secrets converge,
Silent-yearnings swell, emotions surge.
A steadfast heart beats a measured pace,
Longing for love's tender embrace.

In echoes of silence, a promise laid bare,
An unspoken vow, a love to declare.
Through distances vast, beyond what is seen,
Silent-yearnings weave a seamless dream.

Through solitary paths, lonely yet bright,
Guided by hope in the cloak of night.
Love's silent call, steadfast and true,
Yearning for moments meant for two.

In the calm of shadows, visions ignite,
Silent-yearnings bloom, soft in their light.
A journey of hearts, steadfast they burn,
In silent-yearnings, desires return.

Echoes of Her Prayers

In the quiet chapel of the heart's deep fold,
Echoes of her prayers, ancient and bold.
Soft as a whisper, yet strong as a tide,
Reaching the heavens, where angels abide.

Each word a petition, woven in grace,
Seeking solace in God's embrace.
Echoes of resolve in a fervent plea,
A melody of hope, wild and free.

Through the silence of night, prayers ascend,
To realms unseen, where spirits mend.
A mother's love in each hushed sound,
Echoes of her prayers, the soul unbound.

In sacred moments, time seems to still,
With faith as her armor, and iron will.
From dawn till dusk, her spirit lays bare,
Echoes of her prayers, circling the air.

Every sigh a testament, every tear a song,
In the echoes of her prayers, she finds where she belongs.
The world fades away, but her heart remains aware,
Echoes of her prayers, forever in the air.

Blessings in Her Wake

She walks with a grace that cannot be seen,
Leaving blessings behind, pure and serene.
In every step, a kindness unfurls,
Weaving love into the fabric of worlds.

Her smile a beacon in the darkest night,
A touch of warmth, in sorrow's blight.
Through storm and sun, her heart does not break,
Sprinkling blessings in her wake.

When life grows weary, and hearts do ache,
Her presence a balm, for love's own sake.
Through trials met with a gentle caress,
Her blessings, abundant, always impress.

In the tapestry of life, she stitches hope,
Through every valley, and every slope.
Her spirit a flame, a guiding spark,
Leaving blessings, glowing in the dark.

Out of compassion, her blessings pour,
Healing wounds, touching the core.
With every breath, a promise she makes,
Leaving blessings, in her wake.

Seraph's Gentle Murmurs

In the quiet of dawn, whispers sway
Between the silver lining and the clay
Angelic breaths on morning's crest
Cradle the world in serene rest

With every zephyr, a tale unfolds
Of heaven's warmth, in amber bold
Feathers soft, a tender sweep
Guarding dreams in those who sleep

Beneath the stars, their songs are heard
Each note a prayer, each sound a word
In dreams, they dance on twilight's brink
A melody in which hearts sink

In the stillness, where shadows play
Seraphs watch, and softly say
Through sleep and morn and twilight's hue
Their murmurs gently drift to you

With light as pure as morning dew
They weave their love, a vow anew
Guardians' whispers, soft and light
Echoes of heaven, through the night

Eclipsed by Divine Love

Under the veil of the night's embrace
A love divine, through heavens trace
Stars whisper secrets to the moon
In silken silence, a perfect tune

In every shadow, a light concealed
By grace and faith, so gently revealed
Hearts draw near to this embrace
Eclipsed by love, they find their place

No fear can touch this sacred fire
Love's pure whisper, ever higher
In the dark, where doubts may lie
Hope ascends, where heavens sigh

Serenely wrapped in the night's robe
Feel the pulse of the heavenly lobe
Each beat a promise from above
Eclipsed entirely by divine love

With every dawn, love does renew
In rays of gold and skies of blue
Hearts conjoined by this holy gift
In divine eclipse, souls do lift

Songs from the Prayer Room

In hallowed halls where shadows play
Silent hymns begin to sway
With every breath, a hope is spun
A sacred song, the day's begun

Candles there with humble light
Chase away the cloak of night
Each flame a whisper, soft and low
In prayer room, time does slow

Windows covered in stained delight
Filter colors in holy might
Painted scenes of saints so pure
Guide us through, their love ensure

In the quiet, a chorus swells
Echoing through sacred shells
Each note a prayer, each chord a plea
Songs from the room, in spirit free

Come, feel the warmth of every voice
In unity, our hearts rejoice
In prayerful song, we find our flight
Lifted by love, to holy height

Veiled Intercessions

Beneath the moon, a silent quest
In whispered prayers, we seek the best
Veils drawn tight, protect our plea
In sacred night, our hearts decree

Guardian shadows, soft and still
Watch over dreams, and prayers fulfill
In twilight's grace, our hopes converge
Silent voices in darkness merge

Each breath a token, each word a guide
In quiet hope, our fears reside
Veiled behind the cloak of night
Intercessions pure, take flight

Through the whispers, through the sighs
In sacred silence, the spirit flies
Each intercession, a beacon bright
Leading lost souls to the light

In the hush, a gentle thread
Binds our hearts, by love we're led
Veiled voices, yet strength in prayer
Intercessions lift us, ever fair

Gentle Savior's Ally

In quiet moments still and sweet,
Where shadows wane, where heartbeats meet,
A gentle ally stands in light,
A Savior's smile through darkest night.

Beside the weary, whispering calm,
A healing hand, an open palm,
With grace that flows like morning dew,
In every breath, a love so true.

No storm too fierce, no dawn too pale,
For in His arms, we will not fail,
Guardian of souls, serene and kind,
Eternal peace within we find.

When trials darken days ahead,
In whispered prayers, no tear unshed,
His presence soft, a guiding star,
Forever near, though skies afar.

In faith we walk, in hope we rise,
Under the tender, watchful skies,
Our gentle Savior, ever near,
Allies in grace, dispelling fear.

Infinite Belief Hues

In twilight shades and dawning beams,
We paint our hopes, we sketch our dreams,
With colors rich, with skies anew,
Infinite in belief's bright hues.

Through valleys deep and mountains high,
Where eagles soar and spirits fly,
A rainbow whispers through the rain,
Belief's embrace in joy and pain.

Every star that lights the night,
Every dawn that breaks with light,
Carries whispers of the skies,
Infinite in belief that lies.

Brushstrokes of faith in hues divine,
A canvas wide where dreams align,
Each shade a promise, pure and bright,
Infinite love in every sight.

In awe we stand, in humble grace,
In belief's hues, we find our place,
Infinite paths, the heart explores,
In faith's embrace, forevermore.

Litanies for Love

In silent prayers, in whispered dreams,
Where moonlight dances, where hope gleams,
We voice our hearts in litanies,
Each word a love that sets us free.

Through midnight skies and sunlit days,
In every heart, in every phrase,
Love's anthem sings, a timeless tune,
In litanies beneath the moon.

With every breath, with every sigh,
Love's litanies reach to the sky,
In sacred vows, in tender touch,
A symphony that means so much.

No chasm wide, no peak too tall,
In love's embrace, we conquer all,
The melodies of heart and soul,
In litanies, we find our role.

As day breaks through with gentle light,
And stars adorn the velvet night,
We'll sing our love, let spirits rise,
In litanies that never die.

Heartbeat Aligned with Heaven

In every beat, a song divine,
A pulse that reaches love's design,
Aligned with heaven, pure and true,
A rhythm of eternity's view.

Where angels tread on golden streams,
We find the heart of sacred dreams,
Each thump a prayer, each beat a call,
In Heaven's grace, we stand in thrall.

No fear, no sorrow can prevail,
When heartbeats sync with Heaven's tale,
In silent harmony they blend,
A dance of love that knows no end.

With every rise and fall, we trace,
The tender lines of Heaven's grace,
In perfect sync, in sweet accord,
Our hearts in tune with Love's own chord.

Through life's tempestuous, winding way,
In Heaven's light, we'll find our stay,
Heartbeat to heartbeat, hand in hand,
Eternal peace in promised land.

Sacramental Bonds

Threads of gold in twilight's gleam,
Hearts entwined in silent dream,
Whispers carried on the breeze,
Promises as soft as seas.

Covenant of love we mold,
In the cradle, spirits bold,
Timeless vows beneath the stars,
Echoes held in memory's jars.

Here we stand, unbound by time,
Every moment, pure sublime,
Hand in hand, as fate allows,
Beneath the sacred, ancient boughs.

Her Prayers' Embrace

In the quiet of her night,
Candles gleam with mystic light,
Whispered hopes to skies above,
Threads of faith, unspoken love.

Knees that bend on sacred ground,
Seek the strength that can't be found,
Echoes of a heart's soft plea,
Reaching for eternity.

Touched by grace, her spirit soars,
In her prayers, new hope restores,
Wrapped in warmth of divine grace,
Finds her peace in this embrace.

Chant of the Heart

Rhythms in the heart's own hymn,
Rise and fall on love's sweet whim,
Unseen chords in twilight's hue,
Melodies of me and you.

Beats we share beneath the sky,
Unseen symphony, we fly,
Bound by tones that harmonize,
Truths revealed in softened eyes.

Every note a whispered vow,
Carried gently, here and now,
In this chant, our hearts do weave,
Timeless story we believe.

Melodies for His Soul

In the stillness of the night,
Music weaves its tender light,
Haunting notes and gentle strings,
Wrap his soul with angels' wings.

Echoes of a distant song,
Pull his spirit, draw him along,
Every chord a tender kiss,
Moments of transcendent bliss.

In the depths where shadows play,
Melodies do light the way,
Guiding him to peace and rest,
In these harmonies, he's blessed.

Celestial Intercessions

Stars whisper prayers in twilight's hush,
Guiding dreams through night's silent rush.
Luminous threads of fate they weave,
In the vast heavens, our souls believe.

Moonlight dances on wings of grace,
Illuminating love's elusive space.
Angels sing in the ethereal sea,
Their celestial songs setting us free.

Heaven's tapestry, bright and vast,
The intercessions of spirits cast.
In the stardust, wishes find flight,
Through realms of hope, they seek the light.

Seraphim guard the astral streams,
Protecting the sanctity of our dreams.
A silent prayer on a summer's night,
Celestial intercessions, pure and bright.

Beneath the sky, we find our peace,
In cosmic wonders, our hearts release.
Echoes of love in the night sky spread,
With each starfall, a wish is said.

Guardian of His Path

In morning's light, he walks alone,
A guardian's vow engraved in stone.
With steadfast steps, his fate unmasked,
A sacred journey, an eternal task.

The echoes of time guide his way,
In silence, he kneels to pray.
A beacon bright in darkness' grasp,
A spirit strong, with truth he clasps.

With each sunrise, courage abounds,
In whispers of wind, his soul resounds.
Through trials faced and shadows past,
He stands resolute, unsurpassed.

A guardian's heart, fierce yet kind,
In the depths of faith, peace he finds.
Through valleys deep and mountains high,
His purpose clear, to never deny.

Eternal watch, with grace he stands,
Guardian of his path, in God's hands.
A journey blessed by love's soft breath,
Through life's embrace, defying death.

Bound by Divine Hope

In quiet dawn, hope's light unfolds,
A promise kept, in hearts it holds.
Bound by whispers of a sacred vow,
Through tender grace, we take our bow.

Love's embrace in morning's glow,
A bond divine, in faith we grow.
Each trial met with strength anew,
Guided by the hope we pursue.

In shadows cast by doubt's cruel hand,
We rise as one, in faith we stand.
Through tempests fierce and calm seas,
Our hope remains, our spirits at ease.

Eternal light in darkened skies,
A beacon bright where truth lies.
In every heart, a flame to cope,
A life fulfilled, bound by divine hope.

With open hearts, we greet each day,
In love's embrace, we find our way.
A journey blessed with heavens above,
Bound forever by hope and love.

Unseen Hands of Faith

Beneath the stars, in silent night,
Unseen hands guide with gentle might.
Through paths unknown and fields of doubt,
Their faith unseen, turning us about.

Each step we take, a prayer unfurled,
In unseen hands, we trust the world.
Through valleys deep and mountains steep,
In silent faith, our souls they keep.

Guided by love that knows no end,
An unseen force, our hearts commend.
In trials faced and joys embraced,
Unseen hands weave heaven's grace.

In whispered winds and morning dew,
Their sacred touch renews the view.
Through hope and faith, they lead us on,
With unseen strength, our fears are gone.

Unseen hands of faith, so pure,
In their embrace, we find the cure.
A journey blessed by love and trust,
In unseen hands, we place what's just.

Printed in the USA
CPSIA information can be obtained
at www.ICGtesting.com
CBHW071819180724
11673CB00023B/777